I Shot 'em   www.ishotem.com

I Shot 'em   www.ishotem.com

I SHOT 'EM

By

Tyrone Wrice

As told by Mark Anderson

I SHOT 'EM   www.ishotem.com

Copyright

Copyright © 2012 by Tyrone Wrice as told by Mark Anderson

All Rights Reserved. No part of this book may be used or reproduced in any manner without the express written consent of the authors, except as provided by the United States of America copyright laws.

LAST DAYS EDITION: The Man Behind "MAKAVELI The Don Killuminati," the last CD 2Pac recorded

Published by Kram Publishing
Printed in the United States of America

Limits of Liability

This book contains material protected under International and Federal Copyright Laws and Treaties. Any unauthorized reprint or use of this material is prohibited. No part of this book may be reproduced or transmitted in any form or by any means electronic or mechanical, which also includes photocopying, recording, or by any information storage and retrieval system without express written permission from the authors/publisher.

Disclaimer

The information presented in this book represents the sole view of the authors and publisher only. All references to individuals and situations reflect the personal experiences of the authors/publisher, recounted here as accurate to the best of their recall based on their experiences and in no way are meant to defame, demean, or otherwise discredit or impugn actual individuals and events. The authors and the publisher shall in no event be held liable for any loss or other damages, including but not limited to special, incidental, consequential, or other damages.

I Shot 'em   www.ishotem.com

Table of Contents

Introduction

Hip-Hop

Red Rooster

The Mechanical Three

East St. Louis

The First Shots

Reloading

Big City

Evil Proof

In the Restroom Again

Death Row Records

Never Knew

Tupac Signs to Death Row Records

B-Rezell Breakup

The Wack Room

The Last Shots

I SHOT 'EM   www.ishotem.com

Introduction

My story of how, without me knowing, God chose me to prepare the music that would come to symbolize Tupac Shakur's short but strenuous life, full of great disappointment, but yet so inspiring. God's gift to us came in the form of music, coupled with a talented artist who was chosen by God to uplift a generation of people all around the globe to stand up and fight and be willing to die for what they believe in. Death is judged by the spirit of a man. Tupac Shakur's physical presence may be absent, but his spirit will live for decades to come. God works in mysterious ways.

I hope you enjoy the story as much as I enjoyed writing it.

"Hurt-M-Badd," A.K.A. Tyrone Wrice

Words by Mark Anderson

I SHOT 'EM   www.ishotem.com

Hip-Hop

It all started when I was ten or eleven years old. I call it love at first sight, 'cause when I seen this group of guys one day dancing outside my school (it was a Rap), that life-changing moment was when I knew what I was destined to become.

I went to Stevenson Middle School in ST. Louis, Missouri, and after school let out, a group of kids that didn't go to our school always came to hang out at our school and dance. They were a lil' older; maybe freshman or sophomore students from the local high school. I guess they got out a lil' earlier than we did and came to hang out and dance for us as we walked home. These kids'd be outside break dancing, pop locking, and mixing it with the latest dances. Everybody thought they were cool. We looked up to those guys. They're what we called back then "raw" naturals, born to dance.

Every year our school hosted an annual talent show. This year's lineup was stacked with talent, and that dance group came on last. It was almost like being at a Michael Jackson concert; everybody was pumped. As soon as the curtains rose, the whole auditorium rushed the stage. I mean everybody that was sitting down got out of their seat and ran to the front of the stage to see these guys dance. That day is engraved in my memory. I'll never forget. They had on black pants, black shirts, white gloves and white tennis shoes, standing in resemblance of puppets.

Everybody was enthusiastic to see these guys, like they were stars. And I was kinda excited, too; also surprised at how all the girls were so thrilled and eager to get to the front of the auditorium just to see these guys dance. I didn't know that dancing could have this type of impact on people like that. Once I witnessed it, that's when I knew what I wanted to do in life. I forgot the name of their group, but "Big Ups" to "Champ" was one of the members of the group, and "Pop & Rock" was also another member of the group. I will never forget Pop & Rock, 'cause he was the one who taught me how to dance.

Red Rooster

There was this tavern around the corner from my house called the Red Rooster, and on weekends live bands and comedians performed. One night, I put on my Easter suit and snuck out the house and went up to Red Rooster. I found myself outside asking some grownups, "How can I get inside?" I told them I was good dancer.

Everybody was looking at me and saying, "Boy, you need to be at home in the bed, this is not a place for teenagers."

I persisted, and one of the grownups went in and got the manager of the tavern to come out and talk to me. When he came out, I guess he was looking for someone his height; to his surprise it was me. I started pulling on his coat, "Hey, mister."

He looked down at me and said, "Boy, you suppose to be at home in the bed." I told him that I had come to dance at his club. He was like, "I'll go to jail if I let you in here."

I was like, "No, I just came here to dance, just let me dance to one song; you will like me, I promise."

Somehow I got him to let me in the club. He took me to the back of the kitchen. He asked me my name, asked if I had brought something to dance to. I said yeah and gave him my album. So, he took the album to the DJ and told him my name and came back and told me that I was 'coming on after two records, be ready.' I said I was ready, and he said okay.

I started practicing, getting ready. After two records had played, he came back and said, "Okay, you up." So I started walking through the crowd to get to the stage, and all the adults was looking at me like, "What the hell is this lil' boy doing in here? He need to be at home somewhere."

I made it to the stage, and soon as I got there, the DJ started playing my song. I was like, "Hold up, hold up, don't play it yet." I headed toward the DJ booth, 'cause that's where the microphone was. I asked the DJ, "Can I speak on your microphone?"

He looked surprised and said okay. So I grabbed the mic and said with a loud tone, "Hey y'all, my name is Tyrone and I came to get down for y'all. Y'all ready?"

The crowd responded with, "Come on with it!"

I started dancing, and everybody was so amazed at my talent and how well I danced. I heard the crowd screaming. They was throwing money all on the stage. I seen a few twenties, tens, and a lot of dollar bills. The manager of Red Rooster liked me so much, he told me to come back next week.

When I got back home that evening, I had to sneak back through the window, and my mom was right there waiting on me. She turned the light on and ask me, "Where you been"?

I Shot 'em

www.ishotem.com

I said, "I been to Red Rooster dancing."

She said, "I'm gonna ask you one more time, where you been…and why your pockets so fat?"

My pockets was bulging from all the money I had gotten from dancing. Back then, seventy-five dollars was a lot of money. She went in my pockets and got the money out and said, "Boy where you been?"

And before I could say Red Rooster, she slapped me in the mouth. I screamed out, "Mama, I was at Red Rooster dancing."

She grabbed me by my collar and said, 'We about to go up to Red Rooster, and if those people up there say you haven't been there, I'm gonna beat your ass from the club all the way back to the house." On our way to the club, she was looking at me like, 'You gone stick with this lie, huh?'

We made it up to Red Rooster and she requested to speak to the owner, and when the owner came out he said: "Miss, you have something special. I mean, he is like no other child I have ever seen. Your child speaks well and he is so mature for his age. You need to look after him, because he's special and he really has talent, and I would like to have him back at my club next week to dance."

My mom was so amazed at what she was hearing. She was like, "Him, my son?"

And the owner was like, "Yes, him, your son."

My mom start crying and apologized to me, and we went back home.

The Mechanical Three

I never went back up to Red Rooster but ended up dropping out of high school, specifically because of the way people reacted at how I danced. I felt like I didn't need school anymore. Dancing was what I wanted to do, and school didn't offer any dance courses.

I started making my own uniforms and practicing diligently until I perfected my dance moves. I went on a crusade, battling guys, girls and group dancers and entering every dance competition and talent show I could find. I was the best in the neighborhood; everybody knew me. I started my first group called "The Mechanical Three," Big Ups to Troy and his lil' brother Anthony. It was just Troy, Anthony and myself.

One day they told me: "Hey man, look, you take over. If you wanna make uniforms, make the uniforms. If you wanna make the steps, make the steps. We're gonna just be proud to be part of it 'cause we know you can dance." They knew I was beating everybody in the battles.

The opportunity to perform and battle the number one dance group in St. Louis, Shabba-Doo, was presented to us, and we knew that we had to be ready. So I went to the thrift store (a.k.a., the Goodwill store) and bought three black shirts, three black pair of pants, a white sheet and a white lamp shade with tassels. The tassel idea was conceived from the boxer Sugar Ray Leonard. In some of his fights, he wore tassels attached to his boxing shoes, and when he jumped and danced around they shook; it was like eye candy. Sugar Ray Leonard was a great fighter, but the tassels on the shoes made him appear greater.

On the day of the show, we came out dressed as toy soldiers; white hats, white shoes, white gloves to match the white tassels hanging from our black shirts. A lot of people came to the battle that night. Shabba-Doo had a large fan base; they was known around the whole city. But that night belonged to us. The reaction from the audience after seeing our uniforms made me think we had already won. We tore that place down, we put on a show. We had beat the number one group in St. Louis with my dance steps.

I Shot 'em

www.ishotem.com

East St. Louis

One day I was walking home, and this guy by the name of Joe Blow jumped from behind the door of this fish market where he worked and was like, "Hey, yo name Tyrone?"

I was like, "Yeah."

He said, "I wanna dance against you, Tyrone."

I said, "Come on with it."

Joe Blow started dancing, I started dancing; I tore his ass up. But Joe Blow could really dance. I mean, if I really wanted to pick somebody to dance with, it would definitely be Joe Blow, because he was on top of his game, he knew what he was doing. Joe Blow had to be around twenty-six years old. I was just sixteen, but we became friends. Joe Blow introduced me to East St. Louis. The dance clubs and bars stayed open until six and seven in the morning. The clubs in my area closed at 1:00 a.m. Eventually, I would find myself winning every talent show I entered.

At some point I ended up joining this group "R.E.T," "Ready Every Time." They were a DJ group that threw parties everywhere. I got my mom to pay a fee of fifteen dollars a year that would allow me get in every party for free. All the parties were awesome. They would have disco lights, sirens, and every party was packed. At the same time, I was learning how to DJ, how to set up the equipment, how to rent a club, and a lot of other aspects of the entertainment industry.

This guy by the name of Penitentiary seen me dance a few times and became one of my biggest fans. He used to come and get me in the club and ask me to come and dance against guys. One day, Penitentiary said, "Man, you be hurting these fools, you be hurting them bad, you should call your name "Hurt 'em."

I was like, "'Hurt 'em,' that's not a name, that's a phrase."

"Like 'Hurt-M-Badd,'" he said. "You should call yourself ' Hurt-M-Badd.'"

I was like, "What?" The name stuck in my head, and eventually I would go on to name myself "Hurt-M-Badd." It all made sense. When the crowd seen me do my thing, they would say, "Man, I see why you call yourself 'Hurt-M-Badd' 'cause when you get out there, you hurt 'em bad."

My name started becoming popular around the club scene. I was getting in all the clubs and wining all the talent shows that was giving out cash prizes to the first-place winner. Everybody knew who I was. I would be at the mall on Saturdays with my home boys sometimes, and grown ladies would walk up to me, like: "Ain't your name 'Hurt-M-Badd'? Boy, you can really dance! We saw you in East St. Louis, you be getting down!"

My friends couldn't believe it. Here I am, this sixteen year-old with women and men walking up to me asking to shake my hand. A lot of my friends' parents wouldn't allow them to hang around me for the simple fact that I dropped out of school. After a while, I start seeing their parents at the club, and their parents used to walk up to me and be like, "Wow, you could really dance, you're gonna be somebody!"

The First Shots

I met this guy by the name of Fred, who was also a dancer. He was about eighteen years old; cool dude. You could tell that he liked lifting weights, a muscular guy. Fred had all the girls. I remember dancing against a group he was in before and beat them. Somehow we became friends and formed our own group called "Pop and Wavers." Just like all prior groups I was in, we went on to win all the talent shows and dance competitions we entered.

It was time to expand, so we went out to the suburbs of St. Louis to this skating rink called Saints, the home of Nelly and the Saint Lunatics. That was our reason for going out there. We got in the competition. The St. Lunatics didn't show up, but we ended up winning the competition. Fred was a lil' wilder than I was. See, we all smoked marijuana, but Fred would indulge with other drugs. There were times when we were about to go on stage and Fred would say, "Guys, I really need this money for gas, I need money for this, I need money for that," money, money, money. It got to the point where I felt like money was the only thing Fred cared about.

Whatever had brought us together was slowly vanishing. At the same time, pop locking and break dancing was getting old, so I decided to explore other alternatives in the entertainment industry. When I left the group, to my surprise, Fred got a lil' envious of me.

Even though I left the group, I never stopped performing. I continued to enter and win talent shows. Some of the talent shows I won, I had to beat Fred out. After the shows we both competed in, Fred would be very disrespectful, calling out my name, saying things like, "Hurt-M-Badd, lil' soft ass…lil' punk ass, you won…it's all good."

Other people's words really never affected me too much. I was focused, confident in my talent. Plus, I was making money, I was performing, doing shows. Everywhere I went people would be walking up to me, telling me that they came to see me get down. I never went out trying to fight nobody. I wasn't into selling drugs. Enter-tain-ment was all 'Hurt-M-Badd' was about.

My mom used to tell me, "You better watch that boy, he's jealous of you." At that time, I couldn't understand it. Fred had his own car, lived in the suburbs with his parents, and had the whole basement to his self; plus, he had a closet full of clothes. My mama said, "Yeah, but the one thing he don't have that you have is you have something in you that make people like you. People like him because of his material possessions."

I didn't believe my mom. I was like, "Whatever, whatever, whatever."

A lil' time had passed by, and one night I ran into Fred, and he accused me of stealing his car radio. He knew I didn't steal his radio, but he wanted to use that as an excuse to start some negative stuff with me. From that point on, every time I seen Fred, he would say some threatening stuff to me. I had become kinda suspicious and started paying more attention to my surroundings every time I traveled to East St. Louis. It was just a matter of time before Fred tried to pull it, and it was sooner than later.

I ran into Fred in a bathroom at a club one night. He approached me and apologized for falsely accusing me of stealing

I Shot 'em

www.ishotem.com

his car radio. I was like, "Man, you know I didn't steal your radio, you know I wouldn't do that."

Fred was like, "Man, my fault, everything is cool."

As we was walking out the bathroom, Fred sucker punched me. We started fighting. He didn't win, I didn't win, but I did have him in a headlock. I had a cigarette lighter in my pocket that I used to try and burn his Jheri curls. Security guards came and broke us up. They put Fred out the club. That's how much they knew me. They knew I didn't start trouble. I just danced, entertained and made my money. That's all they knew.

Later on that night, my friend came and got me off the dance floor and said Fred and some other guys were outside breaking my car windows. I went outside, tried to play Superman and got jumped on. After I managed to get up off the ground with some help by a few bystanders, I heard Fred say, " I told you, you was a punk."

That really hurt my feelings. That same night I went home and got a gun and ended up shooting Fred four times. I didn't kill him, but I tried too. My mom always told me, "Whenever you fight somebody, you better kill they ass, 'cause if you kill them, you don't have to worry about them coming back, and you don't have to worry about watching yo back."

I shot Fred twice in his back, once in the left shoulder, and once in the back off the neck. The shot to the back of the neck was intended for his head.

Reloading

I turned myself in to the police and was booked on attempted murder charges. I was sentenced to sixteen years in the state penitentiary. Before I got to the penitentiary, guys used to tell me that I was gonna end up joining a gang. Illinois penitentiaries are known for housing notorious gangs. About two years into my sentencing, I was transferred from a maximum prison to a minimum security prison in Vienna, IL, because of my good behavior. There was no jail bars. Grass was everywhere, no fences. They had a skating rink. We were able to go fishing. The only thing I was missing was an Xbox, a car and strip club.

I continued to entertain and organize talent shows every chance I got. My talent attracted one of the biggest names to ever come through the Illinois prison system; Larry Hoover, leader of an organization called Growth and Development. On the streets of the city of Chicago they were called the "Gangster Disciples." Larry was a very humble man, clean-cut, intelligent, and very smart. He didn't look like a leader of a so-called gang. Every day when Larry would see me, I was doing my thang, entertaining. He never seen nor heard of me starting any mess or getting caught up in any drama.

One day, Larry sat me down and asked me was I affiliated with any gangs, and I said no. I started saying to myself, "Okay, here comes the big one, he's about to try and recruit me to be one of his guys."

To my surprise Larry said: "Stay like that, remain as you are; you're not that type of person. You're very talented and you got something good going for yourself."

Before he shared those words with me, I had mad respect for him. Larry had a master's degree. He was a teacher's aide; just a smart, down-to-earth dude. But when he shared those thoughts with me, everything that I heard and previously read about him in the media was secondary. Basically, Larry had proven to me that he was not what the CIA and the FBI labeled him as. Me and Larry became friends, and I'm glad we did. May GOD bless Larry.

I was transferred a second time from Vienna prison to Danville Correctional Center. Danville is a prison for inmates that are about to be released back into society. Before leaving Vienna, Larry asked me was I from St. Louis and was I planning on returning once I got out of jail. I said, "Yes, I'm going back."

Larry said: "That's probably not a good idea; you don't need to return there, because it's too small for what you're trying to do. You should come to Chicago, 'cause it's so big and so many stars come through Chicago."

Larry offered me a place to stay until I could get on my feet. I thought about it for a few weeks and decided to go, called my mom and told her that I wasn't coming back to St. Louis 'cause, "I met a friend from Chicago that's gonna give me an apartment while I pursue my entertainment career."

I Shot 'em   www.ishotem.com

Big City

When I was released from Danville Correctional facility, Larry had a few guys pick me up and drive me to Chicago. My first time seeing the old Sears Tower was an experience I will never forget. The tallest building I had ever seen was the St. Louis Arch, and it was nowhere near as tall as the Sears Tower.

Larry's guys made sure I wanted for nothing. Once I got situated and little familiar with the city, I started looking for newspapers and other publications for talent shows and events offering cash prizes for the winners. Just like in St. Louis, I made a name for myself. But instead of dancing, I was singing songs by artists like Tony Terry, Boyz 2 Men, and the group Mint Condition. I won first place in every talent competition I entered. That was a sign to me that this is what I was made to do. God gave me this gift to share with the world.

I meet this girl and we became cool, started dating, and ended up moving in together; me, her, and her two little girls. That's when I wrote Mr. Hoover and informed him that I was good now and I wouldn't be needing his assistance anymore, 'cause 'I met a girl and we're moving in together.' Larry told me if I needed him, don't hesitate to reach out.

I Shot 'em   www.ishotem.com

Evil Proof

Rainy days appeared and hard times feel upon me. I stopped winning competitions as much, and that created a conflict with me and my girlfriend. One day, she told me that I had to get a job, because she was paying most of the bills. I pitched in every now and then, but she said it wasn't enough to support the family. I explained to her that getting a job was unlikely for me. God had blessed me with this talent and, "This is what I'm gonna continue to do."

She said, "You won't get a job and you have a family, you have mouths to feed, you're less than a man."

God definitely created me to withstand all the harsh criticism and insults I was receiving for choosing to do His will. He had to be with me, because I was always able to accept the negativity and walk away with a smile. The same week we had that conversation, there was a singing contest, and they was giving away a thousand dollars in cash to the winner. When I seen one-thousand dollars for the winner, I went berserk.

Something in my heart wouldn't let me say to myself that I might win. Something was telling me, "You're gonna win; no ifs, ands, or buts, you're gonna win, easy; just go there and be yourself." On the day of the talent show, I was supposed to go look for a job, but I didn't. Instead, I went to the talent show.

The place was packed. I did my thing and ended up winning. That was my first thousand dollars I had ever made. That night, I came home with a sad face, pretending to be mad. My girl said, "You didn't win, huh."

I gave her a lil' smirk and came out my pocket with a thousand dollars in cash, threw it all in the air and said, "You think I'm a looser, I'm a winner; I told you." She jumped up for joy.

From that day forward, we became closer and eventually got married while she was pregnant with my son.

I SHOT 'EM   www.ishotem.com

In the Restroom Again

One night, I was performing at this club called Slick Rick's in Chicago, and this guy Marc McWilliams was there. Marc was a member of R Kelly's first group called "R Kelly and MGM." After the group split up, R Kelly joined a group called" Public Announcement" for a short tenure, and then would become the icon that we know of today. After performing I went to the restroom. I was at the sink washing my hands and Marc was washing his hands. I was looking at him from the corner of my eye, not directly at him but out the side of my eye, watching him starring at me. So I was like, "What's up, guy?"

He was like, "What's up, you what's up; what are you doing in this place?"

I looked at him and said, "I'm in a talent competition, that's what I'm doing here."

Marc said: "No, you don't have any business being here, you need to be in Hollywood, brother. You have the skills of the professionals. You can really, really sing. I've never heard nobody with a voice like yours."

After that, we became friends and eventually would form our first group called "My Urge." That was Marc's name for the group; I never really agreed with it. The group consisted of three of us; George, Marc and me. I was the lead singer.

One day, Marc came over my house and mentioned that he knew Suge Knight, and if we let him hear us sing, he would sign us to his label. Suge Knight was the CEO of Death Row Records, one of the hottest up-and-coming record labels in the world. A couple weeks later, Marc came over to my house with three plane tickets to L.A., with Death Row Records stamped on the envelope. I was blown away, 'cause I had met so many people throughout my journey of pursuing my career that promised me they would get me to California, get me in the studio to record, or they would make sure that I would become somebody. All those promises I was getting from people never came to fruition.

Death Row Records

I finally made it: L.A. Suge had us staying in the La Montrose Hotel in Hollywood, right off Sunset Boulevard. The hotel was plush, top-of-the-line, luxurious living. Whitney Houston, Quincy Jones, and a lot of other stars usually stayed there when they came to town. The next day, we had a meeting with Suge at 3:00 p.m. Suge didn't show up until two the next morning; by that time, we was all sleep. We were awakened by this loud noise coming from a car playing music loud as hell in front of the hotel. I mean, music was really loud for the neighborhood we were staying in.

Marc looked out the window and found out that the car belonged to Suge and started screaming at me and George to get up and clean up, 'cause Suge was on his way up. George hopped up and started putting on his clothes, but I continued laying in the bed. I was the down-to-earth person in the group. I didn't really care who the hell Suge was. All I knew was Suge said he was gonna be here yesterday at 3:00 p.m.; and now it's two in the morning the next day.

"And ya'll want me to get up out of my sleep to do some damn singing?" I told Marc, "I'm not about to clean up and put on some clothes and jump for joy."

When Suge arrived to the room, Marc and George was fully dressed, but I was still in my boxers, a wifebeater and stocking cap. Suge came in, shook our hands and started talking to us, telling us how he was all about his people. He was talking about black people and, "If we're gonna be together, we gotta be down for each other."

Suge listened to us sing, and as I was hitting those high notes, I can see the joy in his face. I blew him away, and Suge eventually signed us as the first R&B group of Death Row Records. The first song we released on the label was called "Horny" under our new group name "B-Rezell." Snoop Dogg heard the song and liked it so much, he paid us to add it to the soundtrack of his new movie, "Murder was the Case," that was due to be released. That soundtrack went on to sell two-million copies. I was officially a platinum artist.

The second song we did was called "Blown Away," which got placed on another big budget film soundtrack, "Above the Rim," starring Tupac Shakur, which also went on to sell two-million copies.

We continued to write songs and prepare for the release of our album. The label had a roster full of stars; Dr. Dre, Snoop Dogg, Nate Dog, Tha Dogg Pound, Lady of Rage, just to name a few. Opportunity was present and the competition was thick. Eventually, Tupac would join Death Row, and the label would become the number one record label in the world.

Never Knew

A few years before I signed a record deal with Death Row Records, me and my girlfriend went to a theater in Chicago and seen this movie called "Poetic Justice," starring Tupac and Janet Jackson. In the movie, Tupac had a cousin who was a music producer that lived in Oakland. Upon Tupac's arrival to his cousin's house, he finds out that his cousin had just been murdered. After the movie, I had this bizarre feeling that I was Tupac's cousin, and I told my girlfriend about the uncanny feeling of being Tupac's cousin.

She was like, "What?"

I said, "Yeah, I feel like I was the one making those beats for him."

She was like, "Boy, you going crazy."

One Saturday morning while living at La Montrose Hotel, I wanted some marijuana but didn't have none. My next-door neighbors who had just recently moved in was bumping their music as usual. Every day I would hear these guys playing music, only instrumentals, and every time I walked past their door I smelled nothing but chronic. So I decided to knock on the door and introduce myself.

I knocked on the door, and one of the guys from the rap group "The Outlawz" answered the door like, "What's up."

He had a look on his face like, 'We do not know you.'

I was like, "Man, I hear the good music, smell the good chronic; can I buy a joint or something?"

They were like, "We don't sell weed."

Then Tupac came to the door. "Lil' short ass," he was like, "we don't know you, homie; we don't even got no weed over here, we don't even know you like that."

So they closed the door and I went back to my room. It was cool.

Tupac Signs to Death Row Records

A few weeks passed by and I got word that Tupac just signed to Death Row. Suge threw a big party at Can Am studio and everybody was there. We all lined up in the hallway welcoming Tupac as he came in. Tupac went down the aisle shaking everybody's hand. And then he came across me, and instantly we both reflected back to the hotel and started smiling.

Can Am stayed packed every day. All the talent that was signed to the label at the time was working hard as hell. The enthusiasm was great, and I was blessed to have access to the whole studio. Tupac started recording "All Eyes on Me," which went on to sell over six-million copies. Death Row Records had became the number one record label in the world, and being an artist on the number one record label in the world came with all kinds of perks. To make a long story short, everywhere we went it was all love.

B-Rezell Breakup

Group members Marc and George came into conflict with Suge. Things got heated and Suge scheduled a meeting with B-Rezell. In the meeting, he confronted Marc and George about some things that were going on that really didn't involve me. I knew my slate was clean. I was never involved in anything negative or unproductive while I was signed to the label. I did nothing but work hard every day and all day on my craft. I had just moved my girl to L.A. She was pregnant with my son, so I was really hoping that whatever the problem was, it could be resolved.

Since I was still on payroll, I was under the impression that Suge would be still issuing checks, but that wasn't the case. One day, I was supposed to receive a check and the check didn't show up. Rent was due and I was really counting on that check, so I ended up calling my manager, Sharitha Knight, which happens to be Suge's wife. I would learn later on in my career that having a manager that was affiliated with the same record label that I was signed to is totally prohibited. But I called her and told her that I didn't receive my check, and she said that I needed to talk to Suge.

I was like, "Talk to Suge?" I never had to talk to Suge in reference to financial matters before, and actually, I didn't even have Suge's number. Suge always communicated with Marc. I didn't know that the problems that Marc and George had with Suge had resulted with Suge dropping the group from the label.

I ended up calling Suge; he answered the phone. I said, "Hey, Suge."

He said, "Who is this?"

I said, "It's Tyrone."

He said: "Who, Tyrone?" like, 'What you doing with my number?'

So I said, "Look, Suge, I didn't get my check."

He said: "Man, y'all fucked up my money. I spent over a million dollars on y'all. We was living plush, we never wanted for nothing."

But I was like why I didn't receive my money. "I didn't have anything to do with what went down with you, Marc and George."

Suge said, "Ooh, you going Hollywood on me." Hollywood meant being a sellout or crossing your homies.

So I was like, "No, I'm not going Hollywood, but whatever conflict you got with them has nothing to do with me."

Suge was like, "What you trying to say?"

I said, "I'm trying to say I want my check."

I Shot 'em

www.ishotem.com

Suge said, "Ooh, you want your money, huh?"

I said, "Yeah," and he said, "Okay, meet at the studio then."

Now, whenever Suge told somebody to meet him at the studio for a meeting, that meant something was going down, and most of the time it ended with somebody getting they ass kicked. Being part of that label for six years, I never witnessed Suge slap somebody around that didn't have it coming to him. And me and Suge never had a problem with each other, but I was still kinda leery.

My girlfriend cried to me not to go to that studio. "You know what happens when Suge says 'let's go to the studio.'"

I told her, "I haven't did anything wrong, I'm in the right, and when I'm not wrong, no man should put they hands on me." So I went to the studio with confidence.

The meeting between me and Suge was supposed to be at 3:00 p.m. I got there on time, but Suge didn't show until two in the morning. I was in the kitchen with my head down; the kitchen was right next to his office. Suge came in, we said "Hey," and then he said, "I'll be right with you in second," as him and about six of his friends proceeded to his office. He took a while to come out, so I dosed off in the meantime.

Suge came out and woke me up, "What's going?"

I said, "Suge, I didn't receive my money for this month, and I don't know what's going on."

Suge walked up to me and stood over me, coming face to face with me, almost touching forehead to forehead, and said, "Your boys fucked off my money, and you're trying to tell me you're not with them."

I said: "I'm not with them. When you say they fucked off your money, I have nothing to do with that. When we signed to the label we signed as singers, and since day one that's all I've done. I been singing and writing since I got down here. That's all I've done."

He couldn't find anything that I did wrong, so he said, "Yeah, but your boys fucked me out of my money."

I said: "Suge, I have nothing to do with that; you know that. Man, if you release me from this label and I have to return to the streets, I'm not gon be shit. I will never be shit, 'cause the streets is not where I belong. I belong right here."

Suge saw how sincere and determined I was. He was like, "So, what you gon do on the label? You don't have a group no more, what you gonna do?"

I said, "Suge, you know I can sing and write my ass off; maybe I can help some of the other artist on the label write their songs."

I SHOT 'EM   www.ishotem.com

Suge said, "Follow me." And I was very skeptical about following Suge, 'cause Can Am had these long, narrow hallways.

So I said, "Suge, where we going, man?"

He was like, "Come on, man."

I stopped and said, "Suge, where we going, man?"

Suge turned around, chuckled and said, "Tyrone, would you come on?"

We ended up at the studio manager's office, and Suge told the studio manager to double my earnings and put me on the payroll as a writer, which was a bad business move on my part. At that time, I had little to no knowledge of the business aspects of the music industry, literally none. But I thanked Suge for understanding and believing in me, and also giving me an opportunity to continue to pursue my career.

We shook hands, and from that day forward I basically lived in the studio. Every day, I would make it to Can Am studio at around eight in the morning and wouldn't leave until two in the morning. A lot of the other artists that were signed to the label, but wasn't getting any attention from the label at the time, would ask me why am I 'always at the studio, your group got dropped from the label.' I wouldn't say nothing. But I always thought to myself that God had me here for a reason. Actually, that made me work even harder. I always felt blessed to be around artists like Dr. Dre, Snoop Dogg, Tha Dogg Pound, and Rage. I knew I wasn't going nowhere. I was determined to make the best out of this second opportunity.

The Wack Room

The studio had an equipment room with a lot of keyboards, drum machines and other musical instruments in it that nobody was using. I asked one of the engineers that I was cool with to help me hook a few of the pieces up, so that I can get some sound. Once he showed me how to do it, I basically lived in there all day, all night. I started making beats and offering them to Snoop and Nate Dogg. One day, Kurupt from the group Tha Dogg Pound took one of my beats, but I never heard the song. Snoop used to peep his head in the room from time to time and encourage me to keep working hard and say things like, "You gon be dope one day." But I always believed that I was already dope. It was just a matter of time before they realized it.

While 2Pac's "Eyes on Me" CD was still climbing the billboard charts, I was working non-stop perfecting my craft. Without me knowing, God was using me to create the songs that would change hip-hop forever. I seen Pac and told him that I make beats, and when he gets a chance come through and listen to a few of them. Pac said, "Cool."

The very next day Pac came through; I'll never forget it. It was around nine in the morning. Pac was a workaholic as well. He worked very, very hard. He was truly dedicated to his craft. That morning, he stuck his head in the room and started bobbing his head to the beat that was playing and said, "Man, this some muthefucking heat right here, this fresh." He asked me did I make the beat, and I was like, "Yeah, that's me."

Pac was like, "No, I mean did you play everything that I hear on this beat?" and I said, "Yeah, this is all me."

Pac said, "Can I have this beat?" and again I said yeah. That turned out to be the song "Blasphemy."

The next day, Pac came in and said, "Let me hear some of your hottest beats." The first beat I played turned out to be one of 2Pac's classic songs, "Hail Mary." No later than ten seconds after I started playing the beat for him he screamed out, "Come with me, Hail Mary, Nigga run quick see, what do we have here now, do you wanna ride or die?"

When I heard him scream that out, I was thinking to myself, "He likes it, but I hope he's not gonna say that on this song," not knowing that God had already predestined Pac to choose the beat. On the third day, Pac and I collaborated on songs "Hold Ya Head" and "Just Like Daddy." On the fourth day, Tupac came in the studio and listened to three more beats, but choosing only two.

The beats Pac chose would become two more classic songs, "Against All Odds" and "Me and My Girlfriend." When I heard the lyrics to the songs, I was blown away. I had never heard that much conviction in the spirit of an artist before. If you listen to what he's talking about and how he's saying it, it would be hard not to think that something big was about to happen.

Out of all the other great producers in the Death Row camp, God chose me to create the music that would become one of the most talked about and controversial recorded CDs of all time. I still get chill bumps when I think about the time one of the engineers that was mixing the song "Hail Mary" came to me and said, "Tyrone, I have never been able to add so much bass to one track."

I Shot 'em   www.ishotem.com

At that time, I really didn't know what he really meant. But what he was really saying was I created something new. The 808s that I used changed the whole game of hip-hop. Almost every song you hear today has an 808 leading the way. And when I added the bells to it, it was undeniable that God had kept me at Death Row Records for a specific reason. All Praise to God.

I Shot 'em   www.ishotem.com

The Last Shots

After superstar producer Dr. Dre's recent departure from the label, during the same time 2Pac was beefing with other big name East Coast rappers, a lot of bad feelings were in the air, and I knew things were about to get really heated at Death Row Records. On August 13th, 1996, 2Pac told me he was planning on starting his own record label, "Makaveli Records," from the proceeds he was to receive from the first single, "To Live And Die In L.A.," released from the Makaveli CD. A month later, he was dead.

I never knew that I would have to shoot somebody for my dreams to become a reality.

I SHOT 'EM					www.ishotem.com

www.ingramcontent.com/pod-product-compliance
Lightning Source LLC
Chambersburg PA
CBHW071346110426
42743CB00043B/2699